NATIONAL GEOGRAPHIC

D0745374

Seven Continents

Elaine Morris

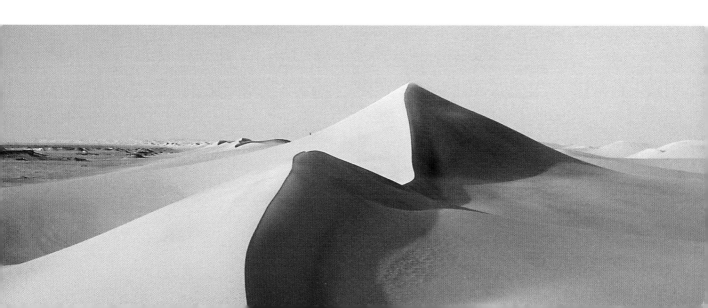

The world has seven continents.
Continents are large pieces of land.
On every continent you will find
something different.

Key

- Africa
- Antarctica
- Asia
- Australia
- Europe
- North America
- South America

2

NORTH AMERICA

EUROPE

ASIA

AFRICA

SOUTH AMERICA

AUSTRALIA

ANTARCTICA

Africa

In Africa you will find the largest desert in the world.

AFRICA

Many animals live in Africa.
You will find elephants and monkeys
on this continent.

Elephant

Monkey

Antarctica

In Antarctica you will find the largest piece of ice in the world.

ANTARCTICA

Many animals live in Antarctica.
You will find seals and penguins on this continent.

Seal

Penguin

Asia

In Asia you will find the highest mountain in the world.

ASIA

Many animals live in Asia.
You will find pandas and tigers on this continent.

Panda

Tiger

Australia

In Australia you will find the largest coral reef in the world.

AUSTRALIA

Many animals live in Australia.
You will find koalas and kangaroos
on this continent.

Koala

Kangaroo

Europe

In Europe you will find the smallest country in the world.

EUROPE

Many animals live in Europe.
You will find reindeers and badgers
on this continent.

Reindeer

Badger

North America

In North America you will find the largest freshwater lake in the world.

NORTH
AMERICA

14

Many animals live in North America.
You will find grizzly bears and eagles
on this continent.

Grizzly bear

Eagle

South America

In South America you will find the largest rain forest in the world. Many animals live in South America. You will find sloths on this continent.

Sloth